HOSPICE HOUSE

HOSPICE HOUSE

Poems

Joanne M. Clarkson

MoonPath Press

Poetry
ISBN 978-1-936657-71-1

Cover art: untitled graphic design by Carolyn Clarkson

Author photo by Carolyn Clarkson

Book design by Tonya Namura, using Minion Pro.

MoonPath Press, an imprint of Concrete Wolf Poetry Series,
is dedicated to publishing the finest poets
living in the U.S. Pacific Northwest.

MoonPath Press
PO Box 445
Tillamook, OR 97141

MoonPathPress@gmail.com

http://MoonPathPress.com

To DeLila Jo Thorpe, RN (1942-2014)
my Nursing and Hospice Mentor,
to my Hospice patients and their caregivers,
and to my husband Jim

With special thanks to my poetry group:
Bridgit, Carol, Wes, Pat, and Thomas, and
my Poetry Sister, Linda.

Table of Contents

III

HOSPICE HOUSE

David and Cecily

*Cecily Saunders founded the concept of Hospice Care
in the 1960's. The seed money was a gift from a patient.*

They were both dying in a different way
that year at the bedside, speaking in dreams.
She, nurse and counselor,
him the one about to leave this life.

This was when he promised her a window,
the place all patients wish for, bed
from which they still could see
the world alive beyond them.

They were in a kind of love, the kind
that lasts a moment of forever.

She confessed her desire to found
a sanctuary for last days, space of peace
where the soul forgives the body
and each sets the other free.
Pain mitigated beyond medicine.

It wasn't the money he willed her,
sizeable, but not a fortune,
that built it. It was their shared
compassion, hers for his suffering,
his for what she had yet to achieve.

They called it Hospice, temple
to last heartbeats that could be a care
home or the patient's own bedroom.

"I will be the window in your home,"
he had told her, clearest mirror
admitting every dimension of light.

I

Vigil

All of them were there outside the window:
    grandmother, lost daughter,
        the farmhouse neighbors. Weather
of darkness and shine. All her longing
    and regret in a single
        final breath.

The miracle was that I saw them too.
    Not features but form,
recognition born of the slope
    of a shoulder, cant of a hand.

Horizon of shadow like a familiar
    Olympic range. The magnified edge
        of a tattered wing. Yes, I knew
them all, by flesh or legend.

And as her body fell still, I heard in my head
    the voices asking if I,
        the newly orphaned daughter,
            wanted to cross over too
as if through softened glass into some
    boundaryless love.

Did I? Did my reciprocal love pass through
    even for an instant? But I am
        mother, wife and neighbor
and must fulfill my years, gathering
    the shadows that will guide me
        through the glass.

Re-Current Dream of Cathleen

You call from the city of your passing,
the city of our birth, with news
of common souls. Sending gifts
I never dare to open. My hand-

me-down sister who lived for only
a month, just enough time to make
a woman. Favoring our mother
the way I wear our father's genes.

You perch beside her on the piano
bench, your light touch arched
over her emotions. I would not be
honest without confessing jealousy.

Your death holds so much guilt
you must be canonized and porcelain,
your future always flawless. My moon
in Gemini, my changeable moon.

When I was a child, I heard you crying
in the night. Then silence. Our mother
never waking. Now that I have lived
beyond all lost footsteps, I still wake
to the grief of an imagined life.

Séance for My Father

She is always with him in every
dream. Sitting obediently in adoration,
the white tip of her black tail alert
as a small, vigilant flame. A shelter
pup he brought home for me
when I was young enough to know
the animal alive in all of us,
excitable and soft. He never taught her
voice commands or hand signals.
The tenderness between them
brought her home, walked beside
him, drank from a silver bowl. The years
after his death she lived like a ghost
next to the homecoming door.
Where I also waited each day
at six o'clock, scent of supper
in the hopeful evening air. Now
that I am so much older than he ever
thought to be, in dreams so deep
everything is believed, I see her first,
frisky mongrel rescued from a cage,
and then the shadow of his firm,
gentle hand caressing her fur,
brushing, tender, against my skin.

The Ragged Phantom

My dream is rattled by a minor key,
    note keener than sorrow
when it strikes during sleep. A single
      howl and then a dozen
        echoing yips—

the black-and-white pup I first remember
    calling, calling home—

the flute, part throat, mostly
    bone, no one knows how to play
      except in loneliness.

I am dreaming about the ruffians
    of this world, the scruff-necked
      wanderers lapping
from the tin plate of the moon.

I have seen a coyote in the wild only
    twice, both times at the crux
      of loss. No pride

of lion, no tribe of wolf. Creature
    old and worn, born for a tune
that makes even stars cover their ears.
      The sweet of strawberry

betrayed by bitter onion. Whistle
    a mongrel might follow.
Mirage of sound older
      than the longest sleep.

Specter

How can there be a moth this time of year
when ice-fall discourages even the steeliest
traveler? But moth she is, worshipping
the blind porchlight, old vagabond fright,
transmogrified from a snowflake's six
exquisite spikes into a ragged pulse death
seems to have forgotten. I cannot put out crumbs
the way I do for birds. She craves light, not sweet.

Sarcasm of soul, butterfly's sepia sister,
she persists, will not sleep or spin. Nudges
the glass of a painful faux-sun until her wings
smolder with the same rhythm as her hunger.
And can I tell a star from a human moon?
What is winter and where has summer gone?

Hospice Swans

for Avril

I never saw the swans
although shadows crossed
the water and clouds
stretched long necks
over grassy acres.
Every year, she told me,
of the thirty her family owned
this land with its spring fed pond,
the trumpeters arrived
at one edge of winter.

Like most patients, she asked
How long do I have?
meaning, *is there any time left*
for one more migration?
Cancer denying clairvoyance,
I nursed what truth I knew.

My task was to listen: to the pulse,
to the breath, to whatever symptom
spoke loudest in the body, hers, nausea.
I smoothed comforting cream
over her thin blue wrist
while asking about swans' voices.
Coo-hoo, she whispered,
Coo-hoo, softer than geese.

And she described how sometimes
only five or six appeared.
Once twenty-seven.
How their down shone white
the way rain makes peace with snow.

I never saw the swans.
Yet in those final hours
I watched her eyelids flutter
over the blue beneath, vision
for the living of what the dying
see: great forms descending
as shadows turn to light.

The Last Piece

When, as a nurse, I visited homes
    of the dying, jigsaw puzzles
were often spread across tables: kitchen,
    coffee, card, bedside.
A thousand pieces a common theme.

I watched a wolf come together
    in the woodlands. An Orca leap
        from the Salish Sea.

"It passes the time," Karl, always cheerful,
    explained as his ragged heart stuttered
then thrummed. "It all makes sense this way,"
    John's wife Nancy told me
since John could no longer speak.

It gave visitors something to explore
    besides grief. They felt useful
finding a splinter of the weathered barn.

I drove boxes of fragments from house to house,
    trading, and never lost a piece
        as I listened to the whining breath
and measured pain on an impossible scale.

Karl gave away every puzzle except
    the wolf. His daughter glued it
to a board, framed it after, tribute
    to small connections
when the greatest was taken away.

Re-defining the Goddess

Mokosh is the Slavic goddess
of dust and steppes. Daughter
of drought and shrines that blow away.
Her symbol is the breast shaped stone

which is why I find her at the ocean
under a wash of colostrum, rocks
swollen and smoothed, pitted
as peasant skin. Deb,

before she died, described every woman's
chest on a scale of eggs: the flat
girl's fried egg, the crone's cracked yolk
hanging viscous above a bowl.
The ovals of sweet-young-things. Hers
were poached. I walk

the metamorphic shoreline, find
green glass so exquisitely sanded
it could only be
from a nymph's figure.

Nobody made Mokosh crystal
or even wrote her story
except on deserts in wind, the way goddesses

come and go: Deb
in her wheelchair in her trailer,
with her earthy sense of humor
re-defining what makes
both legend and prayer.

The Oystermen

for Mavis

Voices below the dying woman's
home. Early morning inlet. Oystermen
row, sharing daily banter. I hear
the splash as they lift and check
seeded nets then ease them down,
the water bitter cold.

On the next beach, her husband
tells me, scavengers hunt
those that break away, bindings freed
by night tides. *I have found
feasts there*, he brags.

My nursing task, I listen for rattling breath,
find her left lung quiet where human
siphons failed. Folding
my stethoscope,
I note a wake still rhythmic,
boats offshore, turning toward their harbor
with tallies and predictions.

Beneath us, four hundred mollusks drift
as if in wombs. While down by the Port
they save white shells in mountains,
ground fine for calcium,
mineral of bone and heartbeat. Each piece,

useful. Beach wares she collected
line windowsills, cupped like porcelain
palms although gestures have left her
and rain is moving in
with the hush of vanished voices.

The Beauty

Her hair was silver, not steel
or nimbus. A polished heirloom.
Patina of leaves after rain.
She admitted her life-long vanity.
My patient, she lived her last days
by the ocean. I do not remember
the names they gave
the failure of her body. Only
her shining, its softness consoling
the aging of her face. And I recall
on that last morning
I combed at her request,
stroke after stroke of river
in rare sunlight. After long winter,
luster where it entered the sea.

Sweet Healing

Everyone has some memory
of honey. I cut a wound-shaped piece
of infused felt and place it gently
on the burn left to fester
for days. The oldest cure
made new. I watch

her facial muscles relax
as the arm agony eases
under the holy fear of bees,

her mind wandering through ninety years
of hollyhock and clover. Even science
isn't sure why it works: nutrient,
antiseptic or simply a second,
golden skin? She lives

alone, with a woman who comes in
once a week to clean, and a neighbor
who found her, forearm inflamed
by teapot steam. And me,

the visiting nurse who wraps gauze
around the terrible, deep
sweetness and promises
to return day after tomorrow
with fireweed, honeysuckle,
an orchard in June.

The Invisible Bruise

Each time I visited, the mother
would point to a place on his skinny arm
and confess, begging me to make her
guilty: *This is where I hit him.*
Then she would weep and weep.

I would give her compassionate facts
that she could not listen to,
as if cancer was a language
as difficult as English. I was sure
she never struck him in anger or rage
or even discipline. Such emotion
wasn't in her, wasn't her custom.
He was her coveted son

who at sixteen fell victim
to pain. And in this borrowed land
whose doctors used lasers and chemistry
to try and cleanse him, she had no
weapon but mother love.

No nurse or chaplain, no interpreter or counselor
could console. Not even the tender hand
of her husband who went out into the forest
daily to gather salal, a refugee's labor.

In those final suffering hours, the mother
showed me again a shrine of folded prayers
then began her litany, *I hit him once…*
Woman whose gods had known nothing but war,
she offered herself as the reason.

The Gymnast

In his forties, cancer returned
for the third time, turning his liver
to stone. Terry had been
strong in the chest
with limbs gravity never tamed.

You can fall, but never fail,
he told me
counting fractures
like merit badges. *Fear
is your friend*, he repeated,
an athlete's mantra.

He medaled in Rings and the Pommel
Horse. Struggled with the Vault.

The first nursing visit,
I couldn't find the door
into his rusted, lopsided trailer.
No admittance
for Hospice.

The second attempt, I discovered
the rickety stairs.

Photos and trophies decorated
one whole wall
across from shelves
of medicines and methadone.

I gambled with: Pain. Fear. Drugs,
he told me.
Scissors. Paper. Stone.

Terry edged toward death again
and again, then back-flipped,
sticking the landing.
Women visited; some out
of kindness, many for a high,
what passed for family.

He hung on,
abdomen distended. No will
to eat, sweating hands
sliding off beam
after beam, admitting, not
defeat, but ease, soul
making wings from broken bone.

Wound Nurse

Skin is my task, my challenge, calling
within my nursing vocation.
My grandmother was a seamstress.
My talent is the mending
within her genes. My patient today:
an 83-year-old woman, living alone,
who fell and could not rise,
who, throughout the night,
crawled across rough carpet
scraping away her skin.

First, I offer assurances,
I am here to help.
She nods her permission.
Gently I cleanse the abrasion
easing out dust and fibers.
Sensing pain, I explain to distract,
salves of honey and silver,
one to feed as the other disinfects,
gifts from a nurturing earth.

Skin is the body, its largest organ.
Others argue the importance
of heart and brain, bone and kidney,
digestive tract. I practice what I
believe, cover the wound
with a non-adhesive pad. Wind
and secure the gauze. Promise to return
tomorrow. But my visit is not complete.

I touch her shoulder, create electricity
between us in the pulsing, vibrant nerves
alive within her dermis. This
is the place where we trust the world

or turn it away. And I know
through working wisdom, nothing
holds the soul like the miracle of skin.

Holding Breath

for Deb

You can stop the breath
but not the heart, the respiratory
therapist told her, offering
some control. Her lungs
were failing, victims of a nerve
disease. He had medications
for that, and machines, exercises
of muscle and mind. Nurse
of comfort, I reached out
into his magic. Everyone

can hold their breath for a time
to survive. Then open wide
both nose and mouth to inhale
the sweetness of wind, the greater
weather. She trusted his cadences;
I trusted his calm tone.
We both breathed easier
those final days.

I still teach myself
in times of helplessness and fear
that the heart can be forgotten
but breathing will obey. Until
we find our final stillness and exhale.

The Difference Between Pigeons and Doves

Outside the downtown library, where books on birds
are numbered in the 630s, a bareheaded man
in a black coat scatters day-old wheat
bread for pigeons. They flock and peck,
jostle in their kindred way. Their necks shine
purple like precious oil. The head librarian

keeps a dove cote at home. A fine mesh net
beds them gently until she releases the dawn.
She feeds them seed as fine as pollen. There is
no comfort like the coo of a mourning dove.

To honor his passing, my brother's Russian
girlfriend rents a cage of twelve doves
and another with a single pigeon. A custom,
she tells me, from her home country. Approaching
sundown, she opens a wire door and the gray
Columbidae soars. I unlatch the second one
and a dozen follow. They circle around
and around above us in white fire
the way bones become smoke. The twelve

disappear westward, while the pigeon flies
south toward the city where a million
votive lights begin their requiem. Where the man
in the black coat finds his alley, settles in,
patient, awaiting the return of wings.

Blue Bicycle Fortune Deck

for Esther

Her cards were pedaled by blue angels.
They rode in the womb of her pocket.
Her cards mocked luck, thumb-worn.
Her cards slept on kitchen shelves and smelled
    of onions and ginger.
The angel on the bicycle was naked.
Her cards seldom fell in love and when they did
    they came with a warning.
Her cards were bartered from gypsies.
Her cards wore overalls not suits.
Her cards were hers the way a cat chooses its own.
Her cards fell into place with an old song
    that didn't quite rhyme.
She preferred sevens and nines.
Spades had the mind of the devil.
Her cards could not cheat, bent corners
    healed by morning.
Her cards ignited dreams.
Truth to her cards was a matter of aces.
Her cards could not be stolen
    even by her sisters.
The nine of cups was her wish card.
The court cards were real people,
    most of them poor.
Her cards were cut by the left hand.
Her cards were born carrying messages.
The night she died they disappeared
    leaving a few blue feathers
      caught in the spokes of the world.

Auditioning Death

My life passes one marker after
another: decades, holy days,
the morning my mother crossed
from need into memory. With each
reminder, I become less fear
and more sigh.

Death, I have seen you tall and strong
offering a chalice of nightshade.
Have looked in the rear-view mirror
and glimpsed you bearing down
chromed and helmeted.

Have felt you at the brink of waterfalls
masquerading as the swan dive
of joy. You shimmy next to me
in five-inch heels outclassing my
blood-red sequins. In many waiting rooms

I have dreaded your army inside me,
ranks of identical warrior goddesses
invading cell after capitulating cell.
I am not morbid, just hooked on endings.
Curious about my nemesis.

Oh Death, you are as beautiful
as an unexpected sunset. Kind hand
holding the door as I stagger through
with brown paper burdens,
the ultimate beckoning.
Aura left after a dreamless sleep.

Twice Silent

Blindfold over the mouth and I am deaf
again. Over years, the music
faded. I was erased from street corner
gossip until only faint sirens
remained. Gradually, I took up lips.

I have always loved to kiss. More nerves
in that blushing skin than anywhere else
in the body. How brilliantly they part
and purse, holding both identity
and fortune. Some might name

the larynx, glorify the tongue, but for me
lips create the emotion of language
and why else would we listen?

Reading their precise vibration, the sense
of sonata returned to me until—
until the Threat occurred. Contagion.
Fatality misted the oxygen between us
and we masked up. Colors and fabric

mock, force me back into stillness,
this second isolation worse than when
my ears gave up bells. All I see
in others' eyes are questions, then pity.
I am deaf twice now.

The Forgotten Field

Today in the market, a word became
    my worst fear. The word
I couldn't find. The one in the small
    pot of thin leaves and brushy
blossoms blazing with a halo of bees.

Scent rougher than spice
    with a sweetness that might be
        lace from a prom dress.

I knew it so well. The name of fields
    we drive by as summer becomes us.
Not yet autumn, my autumn. Coming
        quickly with its soft erasure.

I begged my brain for a simple sound,
    a hint of syllable. I asked my tongue
for savor or twist. I promised myself
        I would not put that flower
            into my basket

until I could name it, boldly present it
    to the cashier, tell her exactly
what I was paying for. I am familiar

with standard memory tests. As a nurse,
    have administered them myself:
three random words to be repeated
        immediately and then again
at farther and farther intervals

of time. Where there was once *key*,
    car, *zebra*, now less than nothing,
a blankness so profound, the mind itself
        is in doubt. My wordlessness

sat on its shelf among sisters the color
    of a bruise on the aging hands
of my neighbor filling thumb-sized
    sachets with the essence of—

lavender, lavender, lavender

Twenty Minutes

in memory of TD

Signs posted down by the docks
warn of the cold current. More than
twenty minutes swimming
can be fatal, they say. This sea knows
life's narrow range,
the planet's caliber. Travis

is famous for diving overboard
after his fellow crabber
washed away in winter seas.
He saved him, treading water
for them both for twenty-two minutes
until the crew hauled them in. Brave

is what we do beyond the body.
In summer they worked
fire lines together, back to back,
remembering the opposite burn.

There are those who test the edges,
jumping just in time as the flaming limb
falls. Time, the lesser measure
of what we call on to survive.

I Promise Not to Tell Her He Is Dying

So much emotion is in these rooms,
walls are weeping. Some call it
steam from soup on the stove. One son
in rain gear goes out to check the roof.
The man in the narrow day bed knows
he is dying. We lock eyes as I coil
my stethoscope back into my nursing bag.
In his gaze I sense a plea. His wife,

also eighty-five, still gets up at 6 a.m.
to pack his lunch although she forgets
in mid-kitchen what bread is for. He
has made one request, not for freedom
from pain or a quick end to breathlessness.
He has asked the same pact of his three
living children and all the grands

and greats. *Don't tell her.* She won't
remember in an hour or a minute.
The threat of death will come over
and over. Terror and grief for both loss
of life and a mind. Deep inside,
she senses something wrong. She worries
her son has lost his job again
or that she has neglected one
of so many birthdays. As soon as next

week, one of the daughters will
have to tell her of his passing. Even this
her fragmented brain won't quite process,
assuming instead he won't be home
from work until late or must be just
down at the store. Or most likely
patching the roof with all this rain running

down her children's faces, slick
on her own cheeks. *Rain* the new name
since she has forgotten what tears are for.

II

When Grief Is Animal

for D.

She didn't get out of bed for a month
after she hit the deer. Her mind
replaying the curve over
and over. The distraction of rain.
When you live near mountains
there is always shadow. Where the narrow
seam took decades to reach
the sea. Coyote country. Cougar kingdom.

The leap was an instant. The impact
endless. She sat in the middle
of the misted road, doe's muzzle
in her lap. The stiff, soft fur. The occasional
spasm of half-life. Last year
her sister. A decade ago, her
mother. The one child
she imagined she could keep.

A deputy arrived and lifted her up.
Some other arms carried her home.
To heal means to dream
until the world is forgiven.

She didn't drive for a year and never
again that road. Some nights she senses
a flank against skin, rising
and fading in familiar animal rhythms:
her sister, fresh from nightmare,
climbing into her bed.
The shadow of a daughter
breathing for an hour
under her penitent hands.

Intimacy of Water

for S.

You kneel and bend over porcelain
into the spray, your lightened hair
darkening into its roots. I am beside you,
worrying water away from
your wounds, made fresh again
in order to heal. So much in life

is contradiction. I am almost
a stranger. The woman next door
who last summer, unaware, entered
your long shadow, the story
of burns: the grill, the spark,
the tinder of your hair. Carefree beauty
flaming into scar. Again

this winter they have incised the healthy
skin of your arms and patched it over
neck and jaw, the crimson shoulder.
I have never heard you mention

pain although it's here, a low radio
of songs familiar from another
life. I massage the shampoo
over your scalp, not looking away
from the empty places, pressing only
my fingertip there. I rinse

and you sigh or maybe it's the water
still quenching. I offer a soft
towel and we wrap you with a crown
of terrycloth. I ease a fold away
from your left ear, flesh surgeons

re-shaped from your thigh that first
winter. A damp strand curls.
I notice the way it belongs.

Glass Midden

I head into wind, combing
rock beds, glass in my hands.
This stretch of beach is kitchen
to forgotten porcelain, shatter
of beverage and clockface.

Everything but bone has fallen
from the cliffs above, a hundred
years past the county's cast-off
acre. I stumble over car
parts and fuses, wood long sailed
or splintered into moon-salt.

I glance over my shoulder, stalked
by a sense of trespass. What do I need
with trinkets of smoothed blue,
root beer, fragment of flower
from a chipped rim? And a century
from today, who will finger

what held my wine, my wild bouquet
of pussy-willow, jar gone to pieces
through carelessness, anger or simply
replacement? Nothing is buried
forever, unearthed and re-imagined
into hand-hewn jewelry or the mosaic
of a frame. My small purse is almost

full. The tide is about to turn. Tonight's
waves re-claim a dowry. I wonder
if she wept when her children's
children gave her plates away?

Snowy Owl

I had no time to go out
into the forest, to hike ranges
of Old Growth. I had no days left
to pursue the rumor of a rare
raptor predicted to visit
our wildlands for hours
or a weekend. I turned off

the highway by the college
onto the Delphi road
where my next patient waited,
her patient husband counted hours,
when I saw amid a stand
of dark evergreen, the utterly white
form. It didn't seem to be among

branches; it seemed superimposed.
Traffic flowing around me,
I drove on with only a glance,
yet the impression was vivid. Even
at eighty feet, maybe more,
I could determine the infinite eyes,
the arctic barbs of feathers.

I could feel in my own chest,
the labor of a long journey
and the winds yet to come. For months
when I turned onto the Delphi,
I glanced into that stand of Douglas fir.
But the owl returned
only in the startle of a dream,

so white the darkness around it
was endless. So still it became
a tatter in the veil. Ominous
but comforting. Even midweek during
ordinary duty — driving, bandaging,
soothing — the northland of a night
bird did not abandon me.

Foxglove

Each June hillsides shiver with them: wildflower
no touch quite fits, rose gauntlet
for bee. Poison made into medicine for
the faltering heart. Ultimately, we all die
of heart failure. If you

pick foxglove blossoms, bring them
in, vase them, they wilt in less
than a day. Never meant to be tamed. I had

a Hospice patient once whose small house
faced the ocean, beach accessed
by wooden stairs collapsing into seagrass. In spring
a vixen birthed four kits beneath that wood. We
watched young foxes chase and roll with tides,
scattering broken shell. What is

poison? The wrong dose? Nature
tainted? Too much juice to force through human
chambers? I wore ordinary gloves
to bathe his weeping wounds. We
lost ground daily as young things
grew, roamed farther up the
shoreline. Summer arrived

with dusty blossoms, even the bees
lazy. On that last morning, I walked out
and picked them anyway, stalk
after weary stalk, favors for a heart at rest,
named for an animal hand.

Requiem for Lillie

Woman in room three, I ease
pillows beneath her, death stalking
a reddened spine, and suddenly
recall a childhood horror:

bones of a horse in a withered
field, less than skeleton. I was too young
to answer the wind that
day. A man's silhouette said,

That's what happens when there's not
enough snow in the mountains.

From this last vantage, the edge
of a peak is white. Clouds travel
fickle as pulse-beats, cirrus
thin. I draw up the sheet,

fold it under her slackened
jaw, count five breaths, a space then
five more, doubting
weather. Terrified, I had bent down

to touch what used to be horse
and saw in that thirst a whole dappled
band, gallop the backbone of sky.

Wild Mercy

The enormous Orca rises, black-
and-white moon from under the sea.
Then the signature symmetry
of a tail fin. Another follows
until a ring of killer whales
explodes and dives before the rocking
tour boat. They have surrounded
a harbor seal, a pod of two adults
and a pair of young, elders
teaching offspring how to hunt.

They breach and disappear.
Rile the water and leave it choppy.
Passengers watch for minutes,
the arc of an hour, without blood.

A child is on board, boy so fresh
he is kin to the wild. His mother tries
to shepherd him away. She fears
hunger might crush him, make him wary
of all he might otherwise love.
His young fingers cling stubbornly
to the rail. His eyes mesmerized
by the seaward carousel. Up and deep.
Dark then dazzling white. He is speaking
with a heart only heartache can imagine.

Suddenly one whale swims off
followed by the others, an ease
of dorsal fins. The seal makes for shore.
No one on board, not captain or voyagers,
has seen this reprieve before.
They sail on toward a further island.
The boy continues his starboard vigil
swaying with the secrets of the sea.

Ex-Army Ranger Saves Teen on Hwy 12

There was this boy
off the road beside the tree.
There was this body that was
a boy among metal.
There was the gash that was
a dark night's cedar.
There was a boy made of
blood and I did
all my training could
to staunch the flood of this boy
to knit him together
with twisted metal and wait
for the scream
of the ambulance. I saw his car
leave the rain of the road.
I saw the exploding trunk
of the enemy tree and trembled
in the ticking silence.
All of a sudden the dream
was real again,
more rain than sand but real.
I was feeling the gaps
in his body, straddling
chrome shrapnel
to make him whole outside the dream.
They say I saved his
life. They want to give me
a medal. I have enough medals
to weigh my body down
in any ocean. There is this
casualty called my life,
one more battlefield,
one more boy.

Following Water

Three years ago, Travis warned us
to take the alder down. Leaning
from among fir and cedar
to menace the back rooms
of our house. During windstorms
its roots tremored the ground
like a bed of venom.

An alder craves sun but follows
moisture, Travis said.

Born in a lumber town,
son of no-one, he grew up
in the woods, could witch water,
see all that writhed
under last year's leaves. He married

our youngest daughter. She had witnessed
his spiked boots scaling two-hundred-
foot trees to trim and top them, placing
a rope. It's been nearly

three years since he knotted
the final braid. And although all of us
traced and tracked every
nerve-path of un-love, no one

really knew why. Today I have the courage
to pay two arborists
to take down the alder whose heavy arms
target our shelter. Travis also told me

he found his way through any forest
by following small streams

since all rivers lead to greater
water. Piece by piece
the pale-barked trunk falls. I gather
forking branches.

Wish Beach

At the edge of tonight's retreating tide,
I find a stone ringed with white
luck. Ancient superstition, the circle.
The puzzle: to find its beginning.
The solution: endlessness. Flaw
of crystal embedded in a marble heart.
Along this shore, rock after rock is banded.

I was taught these rough gems grant
wishes and wishes come in threes: one
for the world, one for another, the last,
personal. I close my eyes, breathe,
cast my piece of palm-sized earth.
Listen for the splash, the hush.

For the greater good, I choose
borderlessness. For another, a body
re-made, pain free. For myself,
the old trick of more wishes. To come
again and again to this beach. To discover
over and over the boundless secret
of a pebble's throw of hope.

How to Build a Bat House

for Barbara

The black careening wind first wedged itself
up under slats of siding
by the front door. His cancer in remission,
she had more time for housekeeping,
was hanging wind chimes when
she sensed their day sleep, examined
streaks of white that smelled almost
sweet. At dusk in their zig-zag

shadow she glimpsed individual faces,
big-eared, buttoned-eyed
with no malice, children they never had,
returning, lost dogs limping home
at the end. *One bat*, she read,

*can eat a thousand mosquitos in one night
or 60 moths. They use echo to make sense
of darkness. Once a year they birth
a single pup that hangs upside down
in the pocket of a womb.* Neighbors

complained as she knew they would,
as though cancer circled their rooftops,
peeking into the sins of their windows,
threatening rabies. Even with her bad hip

and shoulders sore from lifting, she sawed
a square of plywood, roughed the inner
surface, climbed the ladder to nail it firm
the way the diagram described,

as if all her life she had been learning
how to build a bat house just in case
some wild miracle arrived.

Golden

They found each other late,
so late in the dying,
after Hospice searched for someone,
anyone, to be vigilant at the bedside
of a life so long alone.

Lost daughter. Father a dream-life.

Yet when she answered the phone
she not only agreed to drive the thousand
miles, but to bring him back. Home.
A term they never shared together.

The journey for her was field crops
and cities whose small parks
echoed the visitations of childhood.
Slides so high. The breeze
and moan of empty swings.
And in the distance,
shadow of a man holding a toy
either too young or old.

The shadow of this man
so thin, voice so hoarse.

She fed him broth from a spoon,
vision clearer through steam. She dressed
his three wounds the way the nurses
taught her as father and daughter,
redefined touch between them,
humble and tender. Once

they spoke of a golden ball. A floating light
they witnessed together
in a park. Not quite an escaped balloon.
Not quite imagination. Unspoken
goodbye that drifted
into the arc of the setting sun.

The Loon

The autumn his mother lay dying,
    the faithful son kept windows open
toward the sea. You could see it glint
        through cedar and fir. You could
hear it rasp at flood tide although difficult
        to distinguish from the hum

of evergreens. Dementia takes
    a long time. First her brain
forgot her legs, then gestures, finally
            names. The son reported silence
until 3 a.m. when she would begin
        strange vocalizations,

not screams or moans, certainly not
    words. Sound empty of pattern,
inhuman. Visiting nurse, I had no
        comfort but habit. Left instructions
for feeding, bathing, turning that he
        followed with diligence

and tenderness. He kept a radio
    tuned to classical music. She had been
a piano teacher. With each encounter
        I learned a further sentence
of her life—and his. He had been disabled
        by the wrong notch in a falling tree.

A permanent limp and back spasms
    enabled him now to vigil at her
bedside lost among gulls' call
        and the wakes of passing freighters.
One afternoon as I pressed my stethoscope
        to heart and breath, he tapped

my shoulder. *There*, he cried. *Listen.*
   Over the window's worn sill, from
the invisible shoreline, came a cry less throat
     than soul. *A loon*, he told me, her
wakeful howl in the autumn hours
     searching for her mind.

The Old King

for Jess

Rouault's monarch reigns from the wall
across from the sea. The last print
you have chosen to keep. Banished,
he rules a memory of Paris.

You sent your daughter there,
To take a lover, you explain,
in the City of Light.
You, a physician, confide: *She*
died so young. Here, in this kitchen,
of an illness I never knew I carried in my genes.

You turn your head to match the regal
gaze as it queries unpredictable waters. *She*
never told me, you continue, *what her lover*
looked like, what he did for work

or if there really was a lover
beyond the beauty of a city. The tired eye
closes, as Rouault intended. So many
subjects on his mind, so many lost
daughters. Her journey fades

down rues you long to follow,
past cathedrals and brasseries, shops
and monuments. Patchwork king
keeping to shadows, straining to hear
the murmurs of the young.

TBI

What weather can do to the mind. You
were never meant to survive
a slick November highway.
And I have learned that a skull bone
broken sends shards
into the region meant for heart.

You were the gentlest of men. Understood
how aging could lap a curious child.
I knew you as the maker of bird homes
and my maple music box. Until those months
after. The accident remapping
your features, eyes always suspicious.
Traumatic Brain Injury, the doctor
told my mother when you couldn't remember
your only daughter's name. Or the width
to drill the doorway for a sparrow.

Many years later, a nurse, I have consoled
others orphaned by blows to the head,
a bad fall triggering anger and confusion
cocked into curses and a knuckle bone.

Balance can recover. Common phrasing
may return. But you continued to fit the wrong
hum within dovetails, failing fiddlehead maple.

There were moments when your glance
softened and I believed you knew me,
your hands shaping a nest brambled
with affection. The next moment
falling to your sides in fists. To fight
the weather. To grip the wheel. To turn
slow death into seasons built for birdsong.

Cancer Study

The blood is against me. It wants
to live in the veins uninterrupted.
My task is this young man. He
has been told. His father has been told. I
have been told he is dying. Only
his mother refuses to believe.

He is enrolled in a last chance
pharmaceutical study, two poisons
victimizing one young body.
I am to draw his blood twice a day—
noon and midnight—pack it in dry
ice, drive it to a small regional airport.

I took this job because no other nurse
was available and his father pleaded.
I took it because my father
died of cancer so young I was almost
never born. I tell them

I am no expert. Piercing his skin and into
his scarred rolling veins is nearly
beyond me. I inhale. He inhales.
His mother is weeping. I need
to get it on the first stick
or we will all lose confidence
and crumble. Unexpectedly, I think

of my grandmother, an immigrant
girl, a seamstress. I see her calloused
fingertips caressing pale cloth, hemming.
I see her face as she and the needle
become one and I

hit the vein. The life-blood surges
into one tube, then the second.
I had not realized I was holding
my breath. His father is weeping.

I drive through the moonless night
with the impossibly cold package
on the seat beside me. Serum of war,
of pain. Red tide of a young man's fortune.

I Read Her the Gospel of John

This was not about the miracle
of healing although we were there
at the Pool of Bethesda when
the paralytic walked. And we felt
His fingers mix earth and spittle
to lay upon the eyes
of the man whose parents
had not sinned. One day a week
I sat beside her bed
and fulfilled a final wish
with well-worn words. She

was dying of cancer of the throat
and jaw. Even her tongue
had been taken. I was a student
nurse, an older woman,
re-careering into what might still be
my calling if I could face
the ultimate flesh. I volunteered

to visit Galilee with her,
to walk through Samaria
and stop for a drink at the well
of mercy. Even a straw
was impossible for her now. I learned
the wealth of a drop of water,
remnant of wine. We made our way,

my voice, her deep listening,
to Calvary. We became everlasting
companions in those moments
of soldiers and nails. Stood near
a mother who lived beyond her child.

It was the day before
Valentine's when I arrived to begin
Matthew since we had traveled
all the way through John. Her small
bed in the large, hot, noisy facility
empty and re-made like an undisturbed
stone. Had *the word*

taken her home? I was left
hauling in an impossibly great
catch of fish, arms aching,
as a stranger, entirely familiar,
made His shining way across
water. Was she there beside Him
in the whisper of my calling?

Nun Gowns

They vowed poverty so how they afforded
flannel I will never understand.
It had been a month since his death.
We were girls at their school,
sick in the spring from flu
or the aftermath of grief, our mother
working late. A knock.

My sister, wrapped in a blanket,
answered the door. Neighbors had brought
casseroles for weeks while cancer
ate him alive and no one
was ever hungry. Two nuns waited,
still in habit then, shadow
womanhood. They held out brown paper
packages, one for each of us,
even our mother. Invited, they refused
to enter, sensing our shame at the disarray,
scent of sickness no scrubbing could remove.

Once alone, Cathleen and I unfolded
the layers, finding inside
nightgowns of rosebud flannel. Mine
and hers pink; our mother's pale
blue. Floor-length and warm,
stitched by hand, seams of tiny crosses,
buttons of nacre clipped from men's
shirts in the church donation box.

We slipped them over our heads,
surprised at the perfect billowing
fit. Danced like angels spinning,

then together, taking turns
being the bride of someone
we had yet to love. For the first

time in many nights, we slept
the darkness through. In the morning
our mother, sitting with coffee
at the table empty of one chair,
wore the gift of her gown, her body
thin and holy in its shroud of roses.

For Good

An ivory-colored cashmere coat
hung in my grandmother's closet for years,
imprisoned. I would stroke it
like a rare animal. Turn up the hem
to shine the satin lining. She told me
she was saving it *for good*.

She bought it for a friend's wedding,
one she never attended.

I inherited her curse of dressing
only for ordinary days, letting the future
hang pristine. Museum of the beauty-that-might-be.
For if my chance suddenly arrived,
it would vanish without the perfect, spotless gown.

Yes, I have practiced giving in.
Have put on the treasured dress
turning and turning in front of a full-length mirror
with my eyes shut. I am never cured.

My mother buried her in that coat
with its rhinestone buttons. My grandmother
lay serene, vindicated, as if this
was the best time of her life.

Traces

How long do they cling: the heat,
    the pressure, the shed cells?
While I wait for news, I clear
    and clean. Lift the cup
that held your morning coffee.

Since you are left-handed I turn
    the rim that way, place my lips
where yours recently tasted strong,
    hot brew, undiluted.

Is this thirst? I taste not only coffee
    but all the words between us.
What is spoken with emotion never
    completely disappears.

The habit of you is everywhere in this half
    empty room. This time *missing*
is more than foreshadow, foreplay.

Your body is in other hands now. A salvage.
    A surgery. Diagnosis. I refill
your vessel. Sip faith and imagination.
    Drink the fear that might be prayer.

Where You Find Me

for Bliss

Turn at the sea road. Again
by the pasture with three mares
the color of wishes: white,
chestnut, and dun. Turn right
one final time
where someone has painted
a wolf on a mailbox.

On this street
remember the number?
Count apple trees, five
until our sidewalk. Then roses
and yellow pansies.

You will know from a backseat window
or nap on a homeward shoulder.

We never minded rain
or leaves blowing over our shadows.
Come back whenever you need to.
I will not leave even if I have to.

Three mares outlast the seasons,
a new tract of houses: white,
tan, pale green. The wolf
might move to the mountains

but the mailbox calls in a dream
where we are baking, braiding
and reading, humming
the silly old rhymes
in voices hoarse with joy.

Night Shift Nurse

moves from bed to bed
without turning on the light.
This is Hospice,
the final hours
when those who have already
passed come back,
wind through an opening door.

She embodies mother
after mother after mother
　　flawed or kind
　　eager or aloof
some in gowns of music
some with a touch of scent.

Do dry lips whisper *water*
　or *mama*, cool at the rim
　　　of a spoon?

She pauses by the restless ones,
dreaming of thunder
and the shatter of glass.
Replaces sharp-edged memories
with the gift still unwrapped

as the dying one raises thin arms
into empty air
near the embrace of morning.

My sister was my mother,
　　this one confides.
Then I will be your sister,
　　　she replies, smoothing
the worrisome sheet.

She moves with the solace of shadow.
No one is orphan here.

III

Plumes

A friend calls, haunted by feathers,
single fletchings on her doorstep,
quills from the dead. She thinks her mother,
gone four months, is trying to speak,
muffled by sparrow, pigeon,
the relic of a hawk. One is near
the mailbox. Another in spider's web.

There is always unfinished
conversation. Felt, not said. Not even
felt until the loss. My friend's confession
gets caught in her throat: "She was a better
mother than I thought." And "I was
a mocking daughter." Two women

molded by their times and timing. One
intent on nesting. The other fleeing even
her given name. Yesterday my friend
found a white feather on the windshield.
What is the meaning of plume?
"And should I see a psychic or
psychiatrist?" she asks me.

Her mother is ash under a sapling
in the forest. No gravestone but fir.
My friend has purchased a bird feeder
for seed and another one for honey.
Tomorrow her mother may come as a dove.
Or not at all.

When the Saints

She paid healers south
of the border. Burned incense
of resistance. Finally allowed
the infusion of modern poison
in a fatal attempt to out-poison
her own rebel blood.
Today the cottage is in disarray.
Out over water, silver
paves the way for angels who swim
like drowning sailors
above the pain. Those who think
dying is easy have never
been young. Her family
has come, although she continues
to murmur *I am cured*
I am cured. They take
turns at the bedside, a foul
altar. Except one granddaughter
who, at eleven, has the wise
fear never to enter
the room. She stands
at the threshold. Plays "Amazing
Grace" and "When the Saints
Go Marching In" on her
grade-school trumpet. Notes
on the verge of perfect. Some
completely wrong. Most
so sweet they heal
the way breath comes to terms
with time.

The Convict's Mother

I kept a letter written in pencil
on lined paper from a Correctional
Center. From the son of woman
at the end of life. Hospice
Nurse, I tried to get him furloughed
to say goodbye. It was her final
wish. But distance, security,
bureaucracy, the unearned privilege
were too much. We settled
for a call. Him on a wall phone—
they still had land lines there—
my cell held to her ear.

Eyes closed, breath shallow, I knew
she could hear him, her violent
child who stole even her shabby
possessions. Who, I read in her chart,
had struck her once, fracturing her arm.
That man, prisoner of anger,
now sobbed and sobbed. *Sorry.*
Sorry. So Sorry. And to me,
I don't know what to say.
Her stiff, dry lips vibrated with a *V*,
love or maybe *forgive.*
No, definitely *love.*

Then in his voice, they spoke
as one person. She passed
an hour later. And the following week,
his letter. *Thank you*, he had written
and that he had changed, would change.
But even she did not expect
a new man. Only the son he was,
lost outside the way the world says
I love you. Except this once.

The Simian Line

When a child is born, the midwife
pries open the clenched fists
to search with dread for the Simian
Line, a single slash across the palm,
unfortunate carnal sign. It is not

subtle, carves the hand in half.
It can mean reason strangled
or love subsumed, reduced
to barbed wire, as if in its past life
the child climbed from prison
branded forever with pain.

No one is born with unwritten
skin. Each shaken from a bone-bag
of ancestors, path pre-carved
but malleable, ambidextrous. Soon
the mind favors left or right. The non-
dominant hand a gallery of potential
while dominance records every element
of choice. Many palms hold a dozen

lines or more, while Simians
are lone, condemned to the depth
of a primitive stream. I have known
these singletons to become scientists
and linguists, orators, actors—
beggars, and drunks. And I have come

to the palms of the dying when all lines
bleed toward the center, coalesce
beyond logic and love, into a long
remembrance, fate neither animal
nor divine, simply individual.

One Black Feather

for Christine

Her house was full of eagles: black velvet
art, chipped ceramics, coasters, quilts,
photos torn from magazines
tacked to nicotine walls. She reigned
from a sagging sofa, her swollen feet
down where doctors warned
they should never be. White tablets
spilled from a tremoring
fist, morphine, an old, old friend.

Her nurse, I bandaged draining wounds.
Recorded numbers on the pain scale.
Asked if she had eaten. Once
she showed me an eagle brooch. Another
time, a long black feather. *Heritage,*
she told me, her single precious sail.

She coughed up blood. I re-draped
the oxygen line. Days into winter she
faded, field creature caught in a raptor's
eye, the oncoming talon cancer.

The morning she passed, driving
from her trailer, I saw a sky mandala,
two eagles, claws entangled, battled
in mating dance: the plummet, then up-draft,
totems funneling a wing path
for her turbulent journey home.

The Owl Hour

My father holds me in the darkness
with the hush of an owl fluting
through the little fir wood
next to our house. He holds me
against his chest. The buttons
of his shirt leave patterns on my cheek.
My father holds me and the owl.
Above us rides a cloud broken
dipper. It will rain soon
but not now. My father hums
the owl sound. In another room

my mother plays her piano. He rocks me
in time to her fingers. The owl
knows only its own whisper. My father
smells like sawdust and tobacco, the way
I have ever since remembered
the owl, the secret feather of a voice
calling to another voice my father names
as mate. But being a child, I hear
a child's answer from a long time
at play. "I am coming. I am almost home."

Where Does Your Father Sleep?

I cut my teeth on death. The sharp
silence of my blue sister. And then my father,
the builder, no longer loud. So young
and strong that last summer, we had to cross
mountains to get to the place of his birth.

Our house feared sleep the way darkness
becomes its own prophecy. One afternoon

a new girl in my class named Lorena—
I remember the tragedy of her name—
walked home from school with me.
On the way to my room with its single
bed, we passed my mother's
with its twin headboard painted shadow
lavender. *Where does your father
sleep?* she asked me, naïve to the rumor
of our cancer. I had learned fear

well and knew that now she could never
be my friend. *He died*, I told her. Nothing
so true as the absent space
where a King or Queen should be.

And after I showed her the small shelf
of my possessions, she left to run home
to her living family. I smoothed the ocean blue
coverlet over my pillow and wondered,
how could I capture a future
with a pallet of missing dreams?

Suitcase

for the woman in seat 15F

When chance placed us in the tiny confines
of adjacent seats on the crowded flight,
distance lasted long enough for us
to tell each other what we carried
most heavily 32,000 feet
above earth. You related

how your husband, a scientist
of much renown, taught sustainability
around the world: fish streams
next to vegetable rows in Indonesia,
portable container gardens to migrant workers
in the Yucatan. And then

he lost his mind. And replaced it
with anger. You had no choice
but to give him up to strangers
and for the final three years of his life
he never knew your name.

Finally, at the very end
when his brain forgot how to move
his legs and he slept and slept,
you brought him home and Hospice came.
Each morning he thanked you
in his struggling way, saying
I arrived on your doorstep
with only one suitcase
and you let me in.

You weep silently over Texas. It is my
turn now. I begin in the wake
of your courage, opening my front door
to all I thought I had lost.

Phases of Mourning

You changed his sheets a thousand times
those final months. So tired, time became
only phases of night. That he was grateful
you took for granted since slurred words

ran like soup from the left side of his listless
mouth. And then the dying, another term
for absence. He took your stature, your
talent. Your humors, all colors of them.

What does it take to awaken? Pain, certainly,
but also the rejection of your own dance
with death. You plant geraniums on the porch
then walk bareheaded to the mailbox.

You change the sheets for your dreams only.
You learn to live within them.

Unknown Hand

for Dottie

At the edge of the woodlot. In the bed
where I had planned to sow
the peas. A rooted bouquet
of daffodils. Spears with yellow
bonnets. Pioneers in the land of morning

planted by an unknown hand
autumns ago
as a way of making place
courageously lovely. Peas

will come later with their bee-
crazy white fields. The woods will wake
into robins. I see that she painted

only with dream, envisioning
a headstone carved by something
other than winter. Today I bury
my own epitaph. I invite her
into my gloves.

The Grief of Fur

Pets do mourn. A scent. The habit
of a nudge even from someone not always
kind. Even someone neglectful,
forgetful at times of the full bowl.
It's faithfulness that matters.

Waiting for the reunion that always comes
in the heat of sweat wrinkled sheets.
A couch cuddle. Fingers furrowing fur.

This old pup. This graying kitten
lying for the final three days hip-to-hip
with the departing spirit. And then the well-
meaning nurse knocking on eleven doors
to find a new home. A new name.

More plentiful kibble. Yet no one replaces
the first master. Sensed again as it begins
to rain and the silent wind whistles.
A paw lifts as if onto a hidden path.

Waiting by the back door. Alert for the depth
of a certain step. Counting keys.
The hesitant hinge. How love comes later
and later and mostly in the bones these days.
In the faithful ache of the bones.

The Scribe of Time

My friend Wes writes about time.
How to keep it, watch it fly.
How to tell it like a fortune.
I once knew a Mentalist who could turn
back time. To prove his worth

he would choose a date and year, lull
a person into an hypnotic state
and guide them back to a birthday,
wedding, or the ordinariness
of a long forgotten summer morning.

I was astonished when he ferried me
through clocks and beyond. I
not only saw and heard a past moment
but repeated feelings of that day,
the goodbye I had thought final.

And the future? Can Wes, can
the Mentalist, transport us there
into hours not yet born? Is every act
pre-scripted, already shelved
in the Library of Ultimate Biography?

Watch and pulse synchronize at the wrist
while each minute of every day, a cardiac
surgeon somewhere re-plumbs how we love,
the future salvaged if not known,
which is why Wes writes about time.

Sacred

The imprint of a perfect sphere
lies almost hidden in the bleached grasses
of this abandoned field. Each
year it seems to expand a little like a stone's
splash in the weeds of still water.

Some call it Alien. Others the ring
around the ghost of a felled oak. Or merely
mycology, the way fungus arcs outward
from a single spore. It's the exactness

that entices. A galaxy laid flat. When
I step inside I feel the clockwise spin
and then how motion washes inward
and out again along invisible spokes. I

have never known such stillness
and radiance, abandoned like the pasture.
A necessary journey somewhere—or just here.

Night Mare

Her muzzle was gray. They warned me
not to ride her. But she whinnied, nudged me
onto her swayback. Jostled me, plodding,
down to the midnight shore. The wind mourned
in the waves lifting us suddenly like ash.

No saddle, no reins, my fists against her withers,
we sored into starlessness finding places
with unlocked doors where memory
and I could enter. Hallways of lost voices.
My body the age of every tear-streaked mirror.
My mind the thorn of sorrow. Then

we flew over a pasture and the dark mare
set us down. She spoke: "You fed me handfuls
of clover here, so sweet the bees revered it.
This was the best day of my life."

"Yes," I recalled," I was with a dear friend.
The scent of clover lingered on our palms all day
along with the tickle of your muzzle.
It was the best day of my life."

When I woke I was alone, curtains framing
the coat of darkness. In the west a waning
crescent held the hoofprint of the moon.

Bedside

I watched the body give up
its elastic grip. Its hungers dwindling
into sips of tepid water. The eyes,
so full of stories, looking beyond me.

How will I know death? I had asked.
How will I tell for sure? It was like
when I asked the midwife how I would know
labor and she laughed. *You will know.*
You will know. But it wasn't as simple
as that for me, the body struggling
to free itself and now the soul.

The chest rises and stills for a beat, two,
three. Then suddenly inflates, rising
from a deep lake into lamplight.

Yet when it came, I did know. Some bodies
look young again, someone had told me.
Others as old as time can imagine.
All the air in the room had gone. The world
lay naked to ions of traveling starlight.
Even skin breathes, I had never realized.

Until now. No blood, just pale. The final
push as effortful as birth. The letting go
of flesh. Life never wholly mine.
Pain and what to name it. I did wonder
at the end about death. Death itself.
If I was dying. I put my hand
to my chest and felt the heaviness of loss,
the weight of a newborn.

The Found Bone

On the beach I discover a vertebra
slightly too large to be human.
It could be the bone that held
a mythological creature upright.
Or what articulated
the leap of a buck.

I see the space nerves flowed through,
means by which the brain sang
spontaneously and also
with great weighty thought.

It is not quite white. Discolored
by use. More porous than solid,
thieved by both erosion
and the elements of blood.

No other skeletal relic remains
among beach stone, just above
the violence of tide. When I rub
my thumb over its smooth projectile
I sense fear—the victim must have crashed,
pursued, down the brushy bank—
cougar feed here and even bear—
to be trapped by the impartial sea.

All flesh has been licked clean
from this large, awkward bead
awaiting its next thread. One
of a guardian chain that I mirror

in my own flexible spine
as I bend down and replace it
near the wandering grave

of so many animals, some from nearby
fields, some told for centuries
in the starbones of the sky.

The Ultimate Alone

Hospital rules now allow no one
at the bedside. Not wife, not lover.
Pandemic too dangerous to permit
those not critical within the walls
of terminal healing. Death
thought to be transmitted
by touch and breath.

She sits on the edge of a king-sized
bed in a hotel five blocks
away. Watches lips shape fear
on the silent television screen.
She hasn't eaten. Can't cry,
haunted by nebulous loss.

Hours before, she had seen a man
who spoke no English, desperate
to reach his suffering wife, dragged away
by Security. And a woman, sobbing,
forced from her Alzheimers vigil,
the confused husband trying to follow,
falling, not comprehending why
she would leave him after fifty-three years.

There are reasons for rules, the muted voices
on CNN announce: to defend from the spread
of Virus, for the sake of community. She
doesn't believe them, knows he is grieving.

As a hospice nurse used to tell her patients:
*no one dies alone. If family must be
absent, the Old Ones take you home.*
But here in quarantine even angels
have been banned, chapel empty of saints.

No rules get it right without exception.
Predators always isolate prey,
which the virus seems to know.

Through thin hotel walls, she hears
others sighing, ghost steps creaking
from bed to empty window, the worst
fear born in the ultimate alone.

Holyrood

Relic of the true cross.
At the cemetery's entrance
bare wood crossed bare
wood without a body.
When I touched it in dreams,
my hands woke stinging
the way, after a day playing in the forest,
my mother took a needle
and gouged out splinters.

I have no idea
how she paid for that plot
where we buried my father.
His income had been simple
like the hammer on his
headstone. She, who was just my mother,
must have sold something
perhaps something from her mother.

My job was to find the public spigot
and fill the metal cylinder
that fit into his marker
with water so cold
it wept inside out. In summer
we brought iris,
in winter evergreen,
our skin stained with pitch,
the scent of what we cut.

Shivering there, a woman
and her ten-year-old, we never
prayed. Listened instead
to the tomb of wind called *missing*.
She bent and with bare fingers

brushed away grass clippings,
gently, the way she had washed
his body and my hands.

Witness and Healing

for Jim

I have seen the hunger of winter
birds as they perch in evergreen.
Am I healer or merely witness
to the body's casualty? I
saved you by sensing Death's step
and calling traditional magic
to warn his power away. You
are mine through the dark days still.

Our daughter the artist tells us birds
breathe through their bones
where light and music meet,
where wings and weather survive together.

I have seen the skeleton of the devil
and faced him into dust.

Our daughter sketches the fossil
of a sparrow, its intricate symmetry
revealing how muscles
create each species of motion. We
breathe. We breathe together through
worn bones where desire
and helplessness collide
in a heart the size of a wren. I have seen
how winter feeds the birds.
I am learning the rescue of witness.

The Art of Dying

for Jess

Your son doesn't believe when you claim
everything repeats and you know outcomes
of novels and Sunday's ball game.
You see him mouth 'dementia' when he thinks

you can't see. You've read his lips
for years through cataracts. It isn't what you've
forgotten that disturbs. It's all you remember,
moments folded and re-folded until every word

bleeds through. One day of a hundred-
and-one years is nothing compared with the pulse
of an hour. Medical personnel keep lotteries
on your passing, disease testifying against you.

Only you realize Death does not count
but inscribes infinity, suffering skating into
twin ovals of joy. Life, the ceremony
of reflective water over a shining stone. Blush

of spectrums emerging from blue. Your comfort:
symphony, sweet symmetries fitting the opening
soul. This ache mislabeled angina. You know
Beethoven beyond tide or daylight. Art

is never true until the perfect repetition. You
assure me love will be easier soon. I will
find you with every breath already, next to me
now, then suddenly within.

Acknowledgements

Grateful appreciation to the editors of the following journals where poems previously appeared:

American Journal of Nursing (AJN): "Intimacy of Water" and "I Promise Not to Tell Her He Is Dying"

Bacopa Literary Review: "Auditioning Death"

Bellingham Review: "The Art of Dying"

Calyx: "For Good"

Creative Colloquy: "Where You Find Me"

Crosswinds: "The Found Bone"

Faultline: "Plumes" and "Traces"

HEAL: Humanism Evolving through Arts and Literature: "Wound Nurse"

Heartland Review: "Twice Silent"

Leaping Clear: "How to Build a Bat House"

Medical Literary Messenger: "The Beauty" and "The Loon"

Mom Egg Review: "Night Shift Nurse"

Months to Years: "Hospice Swans"

Natural Bridge: "The Difference Between Pigeons and Doves"

Painted Bride Quarterly: "Re-Current Dream of Cathleen"

Panolply: "The Simian Line"

Passager: "Sacred"

Paterson Literary Review: "Suitcase" and "Nun Gowns"

Pensive: "Snowy Owl"

Poeming Pigeon: In the News Anthology: "Ex-Army Ranger Saves Teen on Hwy 12"

Poetry Northwest, Joan Swift Memorial Prize Finalist: "The Oystermen"

Rockvale Review: "The Owl Hour"

Sheila-Na-Gig: "Blue Bicycle Fortune Deck"

Snapdragon, A Journal of Art and Healing: "Requiem for Lillie" and "When the Saints"

Split Rock Review: "Glass Midden"

Switchgrass Review: "One Black Feather"

Talking River Review: "Twenty Minutes"

The Healing Muse: "The Last Piece"

The Tishman Review: "Holyrood"

Tor House, Robinson Jeffers Prize, Honorable Mention 2020: "When Grief Is Animal"

The Westchester Review: "Wish Beach"

We'Moon: "Night Mare"

Zone 3: "Following Water"

About the Author

Joanne M. Clarkson fell in love with poetry as a child and it has been a life-long relationship. Her favorite poem, at 10, was "The Highwayman" by Alfred Noyes. She won her first poetry contest in fifth grade with rhyming verse about Mt. Rainier. Since then, she has had a thousand favorite poems and has published many of her own. Her fifth collection, *The Fates*, won Bright Hill Press' annual contest and was published in 2017. She has received a Grant for Artist Progress (GAP) from Artist Trust and was awarded an NEH Poetry in Person Grant to teach poetry in rural libraries.

Clarkson has Master's Degrees in English and Library and Information Science. She taught and then worked as a professional librarian for many years. After caring for her mother through a long illness she re-careered as a Registered Nurse, specializing in Home Health and Hospice. Her memoir, *There's Always a Miracle: True Stories of Life Before and After Death* (Black Triangle Press, 2022), includes chapters from her personal life and her hospice work.

Besides poetry, her life-long avocation has been reading palms and Tarot. She was taught by her grandmother, psychic Esther Monson. She continues to give personal readings and classes and to add mystical moments to events and celebrations.

Clarkson lives with her husband James in Port Townsend, WA. She loves spending time with family, including 5 children and 4 grandchildren. She gardens and she and her husband avidly dance Argentine Tango.